CHILDREN'S
ENCYCLOPEDIA
OF PREDATORS

Alex Woolf and Claire Philip

ARCTURUS

Picture Credits:
Every attempt has been made to clear copyright. Should there be any inadvertent omission,
please apply to the publisher for rectification.
Key: b-bottom, t-top, c-center, l-left, r-right

All images Shutterstock
1 KarenGiblettPhotography, 4-5c FPWing , 4 t Scott E Read, , 4c Carlos Grillo , 4b underworld , 5t Kurit afshen, 5c Vlada Cech, 5b Milan Zygmunt, 6-7c juancarcha69 , 6b UNGSUK KO, 7t Menno Schaefer , 8-9c Wildpix productions , 8l A.von Dueren , 8r Timothy Stringer, 10-11c Jaroslav Moravcik, 10bl Holly Kuchera, 11cr WildMedia, 12-13c Warren Metcalf, 12c Jim Cumming, 13b Chris Desborough, 14-15c Ondrej Prosicky , 14c Ondrej Prosicky, 15c Henrico Muller, 16-17c Scott E Read, 16b Kelp Grizzly Photography, 17t Sergey Uryadnikov., 18-19c WildMedia, 18b Giedriius., 19c miroslav chytil, 20-21c Scott E Read, 20cl Richard Seeley, 21tr Byron Layton, 22-23 cr Antoni Murcia , 22bl Martin Rudlof Photography, 22c Greg and Jan Ritchie, 24-25c Laura Hedien , 24bl Graham Bloomfield, 25 cr bobby20, 26-27c Betty Shelton, 26bc Debbie Steinhausser, 27tr nialat, 28-29c Alexandre Boudet, 28b Steve Boer, 29cr Sketchart, 30-31c Alexey Seafarer, 30bl Sylvie Bouchard, 31tr evaurban, 32-33c Christopher Wood., 32bl Tyler Olson, 33tr GTW, 34-35c Tigger11th, 34bl vanchai, 35tR APIWICH PUDSUMRAN, 36-37c Volodymyr Burdiak, 36bl Jeff Cable Photography, 37tr Dennis W Donohue, 38-39c Lennjo, 38bl zhenya, 39tr Volodymyr Burdiak, 40-41c Maggy Meyer, 40c benoit_f, 41t Catchlight Lens, 42-43c mina adel cr7, 42b Setta Sornnoi, 43tl hxdbzxy, 44-45c Jim Cumming, 44cl Alan Jeffery, 45cr GUDKOV ANDREY, 46-47c Maggy Meyer, 46cl Hemant Surti, 47tl Maggy Meyer, 48-49c Maggy Meyer, 48cl LauraDyer, 49b Stu Porter, 50-51c Uwe Bergwitz, 50c Nando, 51tr Anton Ivanov, 52-53c Hans Wagemaker, 52bl Gurkan Ozturk, 53br dean bertoncelj, 54-55c Geoffrey Kuchera, 54c Melanie DeFazio, 55c Tony Rix, 56-57c Stu Porter, 56bc Viju Jose, 57tr Vaganundo_Che, 58-59c Dennis W Donohue, 58bl slowmotiongli, 59c Chris Desborough, 60-61c slowmotiongli, 60cb Tomas Hulik ARTpoint, 61tr Xavier Balmes Broton, 62-63c wildestanimal, 62cl photobar, 63cr Martin Mecnarowski, 64-65c Cheri Alguire, 65tr worldswildlifewonders, 65bl J. Norman Reid, 66-67c diegooscar01, 66bl benoit_f, 67bc GUDKOV ANDREY, 68-69c Bernhard Richter, 68bc Ohmega1982, 69tr Four Oaks, 70-71c sushil kumudini chikane, 70bl TravellingFatman, 71tl sven.bernet, 72-73c Heiko Kiera, 72bl Tony Campbell, 73cr Paul S. Wolf, 74-75c Vladislav T. Jirousek, 74cl Marek Velechovsky, 75cr Danny Ye, 76-77c Tanguy de Saint-Cyr, 76cl Danny Ye., 77cr Uwe Bergwitz, 78-79c Ramon Carretero, 78bl Alessandro De Maddalena, 79br BW Folsom, 80-81c Zi Magine, 80cl Sergey Uryadnikov, 81bl Alberto Carrera, 82-83c Tomas Kotouc, 82bl Tony Campbell., 83tl Ramon Carretero, 84-85c Matt9122, 84bc Love Lego, 85tr Matthew R McClure, 86-87c Tomas Kotouc, 86bl Matt9122, 87cr le bouil baptiste, 88-89c Martin Prochazkacz, 88cl Gelia., 89tl Martin Prochazkacz, 90-91c Maui Topical Images, 90bl Greg Amptman, 91ct Fiona Ayerst, 92-93c wildestanimal, 92bl Tomas Kotouc., 93br Alessandro De Maddalena, 94-95c Alessandro De Maddalena, 94bl Alessandro De Maddalena, 95tr lunamarina, 96-97c GHughesPhoto, 96bl Aaronejbull87, 97t martin_hristov, 98-99c nicolasvoisin44, 98l Brandelet, 99r Alex Rush, 100-101c David Havel, 100bl Eric Isselee, 100t Enrique Ramos, 102-103c sukanya sitthikongsak, 102c Eugene Troskie, 102b stalk, 104-105c Nathan A Shepard, 104cl Dr Morley Read, 105t Radiant Reptilia., 106-107c Glenn McCrea, 106c Maria Dryfhout, 107tr MSMondadori, 108-109c Natalia Kuzmina, 108cl Hannamariah, 109br Jan Hejda, 110-111c ShutterOK, 110bl Colette3, 111br chamleunejai, 112-113c Danny Ye, 112bl Gulliver20, 113br Heiko Kiera, 114-115c Milan Zygmunt, 114c fendercapture, 114bl nstermo, 116-117c Jeff W. Jarrett, 116bl Ernie Cooper, 117br KarenGiblettPhotography, 118-119c Ken Griffiths, 118bc Pong Wira, 119tr Pong Wira, 120-121c reisegraf.ch, 120cl shunfa Teh, 121bl Ryan M. Bolton, 122-123c Vince Adam, 122b Ken Griffiths, 123br IJPhoto, 124-125c Jeff Holcombe, 124cr Dr Morley Read, 124bl zaidi razak
Front cover main image Ondrej Prosicky, tll Kurit afshen, tl Vaclav Sebek, c Ken Kiefer, cr Anna Levan, crr Audrey Snider-Bell; back cover Vlada Cech.

ARCTURUS

This edition published in 2022 by Arcturus Publishing Limited
26/27 Bickels Yard, 151–153 Bermondsey Street,
London SE1 3HA

Copyright © Arcturus Holdings Limited

Authors: Alex Woolf and Claire Philip
Designer: Lorraine Inglis
Picture research: Lorraine Inglis and Paul Futcher
Editor: Becca Clunes
Design manager: Jessica Holliland
Managing editor: Joe Harris

ISBN: 978-1-3988-1459-2
CH010143NT
Supplier 29, Date 0622, Print run 00001922

Printed in China

CHILDREN'S
ENCYCLOPEDIA
OF PREDATORS

CONTENTS

Introduction

Predators are wild animals that hunt other animals for food. They have all developed special ways to catch and kill their prey. Some, like wolves, work together in packs, while others have adaptations, such as venomous fangs, to ensure they get a meal.

Big Beasts

Big and bulky, bears have huge claws and sharp teeth to help them catch and kill prey. These animals can be incredibly fierce, yet most are omnivores, meaning they eat plants as well as insects, fish, and other animals.

Bears are apex predators, which means that no other animal hunts them.

Super Sharks

Sharks are some of the most efficient hunters on Earth. They have incredibly developed senses, which help them to detect their prey. Different species hunt in various ways. For example, some pin animals to the sea floor, while others snap and grab with a deadly bite.

Crocodiles can open their mouth very wide to swallow their prey whole.

Many sharks circle their prey before moving in to strike.

Dangerous Reptiles

Crocodiles and alligators hunt their prey by ambushing it from the water's edge. They then drag it down below the surface to drown it before taking large mouthfuls.

Spectacular Snakes

Snakes can track and attack animals by sensing their body heat and by smelling them. Once caught, prey is eaten live and swallowed whole.

Some snakes use venom to kill their prey, while others squeeze them to death.

Clever Canids

Members of the dog family often hunt in packs or in pairs. They will follow their prey, looking for a weak animal to pounce on.

Deadly Spiders

Some spiders sit and wait for prey to pass by, while others run around, actively seeking insects to eat. After capturing prey, most spiders will use venom to subdue it.

A spider's fangs are hollow, like needles. The spider bites its prey to inject venom.

Canids

One group of predators may seem very familiar to you. The canid family includes domestic dogs, as well as wolves, foxes, jackals, and several types of wild dog. They are all meat-eaters with strong jaws and sharp teeth.

Big and Small

Canids come in all sizes but have many common features. The smallest is the fennec fox, found in Africa. The largest is the timber wolf. Canids are hunters with a strong sense of smell and good hearing. They have a furry body, legs designed for running long distances, and paws with claws on each toe.

Members of the canid family are found on every continent except Antarctica. They were introduced to Australia by humans about 5,000 years ago.

The tiny fennec fox weighs less than a family bottle of cola. Its large ears help it to stay cool in the desert heat.

Family Values

Many types of wild canid live in social groups, although some only get together to breed. Their young are called pups, cubs, or kits. They have several pups in one litter and feed them on their milk until they are big enough to eat meat.

Some canids have patterned fur, but most have plain fur with no spots or stripes.

Canids like these wolves communicate with scent signals but also with noises such as barks, growls, and howls.

Canids are "digitigrade," which means they walk on their toes, rather than on their whole foot.

DID YOU KNOW? Canids can't sweat, so they lose heat through their nose and mouth— that's why dogs pant when they are hot.

Wolves

The wolf is the largest member of the canid family, yet unlike its dog relatives, it is undomesticated. Wolves live in the wild in remote areas across North America, Europe, and Asia. Although wolves used to roam far and wide, today their numbers are dwindling.

A wolf's long snout gives it an excellent sense of smell, which it uses to track down its prey.

Wolf Pups

Wolves mate between January and March each year. Around nine weeks later, a litter of up to 11 pups is born. At first, the pups cannot see or hear and are entirely dependent on their mother.

They drink her milk until some time between three and ten weeks, when they begin to eat regurgitated meat. The pups start to hunt prey at around six months old.

Wolves have extremely sharp teeth, which they use to take down their prey.

Family Groups

Wolves live in family groups called packs. The pack is usually made up of parents, cubs, and older offspring. Only the parents mate and produce young, yet all the wolves help feed and raise the pups.

One of the ways wolves communicate with their pack is howling.

DID YOU KNOW? A wolf may roll on its back or crouch low to the ground to show it is submissive to another wolf.

A wolf's coat is made up of a water-resistant outer layer and an inner layer of thick fur.

A pack of wolves will often chase their prey for long distances before they are able to strke successfully.

TIMBER WOLF

CANIS LUPUS

Habitat: Forests, grasslands, mountains, deserts, tundra; North America, Europe, Asia, and parts of the Middle East
Length: Up to 1.80 m (6 ft)
Weight: 34–50 kg (75–110 lb)
Diet: Deer, bison, moose, beavers, rodents, hares, birds
Lifespan: 6–13 years

Red Foxes

This striking creature is found in more places around the globe than any other carnivorous mammal. They adapt to all kinds of habitats and will eat eggs, plants, and insects if they can't catch fresh meat.

Long whiskers and excellent night vision help the red fox to hunt in the dark.

A male fox is called a dog and makes a barking sound. The female is called a vixen and makes a blood–curdling screaming noise.

Home Sweet Home

A red fox's home is called a den, burrow, or earth. They are often found on the edge of a field or forest, with plenty of hunting ground nearby. The fox digs its own den, or takes over a den from another animal. The fox will store food in these underground tunnels, and use them to keep their young safe.

Adult foxes are rarely hunted by other animals, although they may be attacked by predators such as wolves and coyotes.

Habitat: Forests, grasslands, mountains, urban areas; North America, Europe, Asia, and parts of North Africa
Length: Up to 1.4 m (4.5 ft)
Weight: 3–11 kg (6.5–24 lb)
Diet: Plants, nuts, berries, and roots as well as small mammals, birds, frogs, worms, insects, and human scraps
Lifespan: 2–4 years

A red fox leaves a scent trail with its paws so it can follow familiar paths each night.

Super Sense

Smell is very important to a fox. It has special glands on its face, feet, and tail that produce a smelly substance used for scent-marking its territory. It also communicates with scent messages from its urine and poop, left around trees and rocks.

The long, bushy tail is called a "brush" and helps the fox to balance and send signals to other foxes.

Coyotes

Sometimes known as the prairie wolf, the coyote is found as far north as Canada and Alaska, and as far south as Costa Rica and Panama. They are more closely related to wolves, jackals, and dogs than they are to other canids.

They look wolf-like, but coyotes differ from wolves because they willingly hunt on their own. For larger prey, though, coyotes will hunt in a pack.

Furred Feet

Coyotes, in common with many other canids, have non-retractable claws on their toes. This means that the claws are permanently touching the ground to give them grip when they run. (Some carnivores, including foxes and big cats, can pull their claws in to protect them.) A coyote's front feet have four claws that touch the ground, and a smaller dew claw at the back which does not come into contact with the ground.

A coyote's fur can be a mixture of red, brown, tan, and yellow, with white underparts.

COYOTE

CANIS LATRANS

Habitat: Forests, grasslands, deserts, swamps, urban areas; North and Central America
Length: Up to 1.2 m (4 ft)
Weight: 9–23 kg (20–50 lb)
Diet: Small mammals, deer, some birds, snakes, carrion, fruits, berries, and vegetables
Lifespan: Up to 10 years

In the wild, coyotes are preyed upon by wolves, bears, and mountain lions.

Hear My Voice

You may hear a coyote even if you can't see one—they are very vocal creatures. They communicate with whines, howls, yips, growls, and barks. A high-pitched bark is used to call to pups, while a short bark means danger. A long howl tells other coyotes where the caller is.

The young grow quickly, reaching their full size in just a year (compared to two years for a wolf).

Coyotes are monogamous, which means they stay with the same breeding partner for several years.

DID YOU KNOW? A coyote generally runs with its tail pointing down to the ground. A wolf holds its tail horizontally as it runs, while dogs often keep theirs pointing upward when they run.

Painted Wolves

Also known as African wild dogs, painted dogs, Cape hunting dogs, and African hunting dogs, these animals have beautiful patterned fur and large, round ears. They live in closely bonded family groups known as packs.

Alpha Female

A pack is led by a female leader and her male partner. They are the alpha pair and will usually be the only ones who breed. The alpha female decides where the pack will hunt, when they will hunt and when they will rest, and what they will try to catch.

The painted wolf has the strongest bite, for its body size, of any living carnivore.

A pack needs six adults to hunt and breed successfully, but some packs are much bigger than that.

PAINTED WOLF

LYCAON PICTUS

Habitat: Plains and woodlands; Eastern and Southern Africa
Length: 1–1.5 m (3–5 ft)
Weight: 18–36 kg (40–80 lb)
Diet: Antelopes, warthogs, hares, rodents
Lifespan: Up to 11 years

Adults feed on a kill but regurgitate some of the meat back at the den, for the pups to eat.

Like other canid pups, these ones are born blind and helpless.

Pack Mentality

Scientists studying packs of painted wolves have noticed how strong their bond is. The pack will look after elderly, sick, or injured members and will not leave them behind. They bring them food and try to nurse them back to full strength where possible. They reinforce their bonds by licking, smelling, and rubbing against each other.

Painted wolves can run for hours following their prey.

Bears

Despite their cuddly "teddy bear" image, bears are impressive beasts. Their huge size and strength combined with sharp teeth and claws make them formidable hunters.

Huge Appetite

Bears are found worldwide and there are eight species—brown bears, Asiatic black bears, North American black bears, giant pandas, polar bears, spectacled bears, sloth bears, and sun bears. Bears feed on animals and fish, but they also search for fruit, plants, seeds, eggs, insects, and carrion (meat that is already dead).

A full-throated bear roar—one of nature's more awesome sights and sounds!

On the Move!

Although they usually move quite slowly, bears can actually run very fast—up to 56 km/h (35 mph)— which is extremely useful when chasing down prey!

This bear has picked up its pace to chase its prey.

DID YOU KNOW? Bears are one of the few animals that eat honey. They use their strong paws to rip open beehives while their thick fur protects them from stings.

A bear has better hearing than a human. It also has an extremely sensitive nose. It uses its sense of smell to sniff out food, other bears, and anything dangerous, from miles away.

Bears kill large animals, such as moose, by using their claws to pull their prey down and then biting their neck or spine.

All bears have non-retractable claws and a large, stocky body.

Brown Bears

The brown bear is the most well known of all bear species. It is found in many different parts of the world, especially in isolated mountain regions and dense forests.

Preparing for Winter

Brown bears are omnivores—meaning they like to eat all kinds of food, especially fish, birds, mammals, carrion, roots, berries, and herbs. They will eat great quantities in the months leading up to winter, when they enter a long deep sleep that lasts until spring. When they wake, they will have lost much of their bodyweight.

Brown bears will stand up on their hind legs to see better.

Brown bear cubs live with their mother until they are around three years old.

DID YOU KNOW? Brown bears tend to be crepuscular (most active at dawn and dusk) but many become nocturnal if they live near to humans.

You can spot a brown bear from its shoulder hump—a large mass of muscle that helps it dig up roots, move rocks, and tear apart logs to find food.

Hungry Hunters

Brown bears often steal the kills of other predators, such as wolves. The bigger bears hunt large mammals such as moose and caribou.

The largest brown bears of all live in coastal areas where they feed on protein-rich salmon in preparation for a long winter.

Brown bears will dive into the water to pin down and catch fish.

Brown bear cubs face many dangers from predators— including some adult male bears!

BROWN BEAR

URSUS ARCTOS

Habitat: Forests, grasslands, mountains; North America, Europe, and Asia
Length: Up to 2.8 m (9 ft)
Weight: 80–600 kg (170–1,300 lb)
Diet: Plants, nuts, berries, and roots as well as deer, beaver, caribou, salmon, small reptiles, amphibians
Lifespan: Up to 30 years

Grizzly Bears

The grizzly is a type of brown bear and one of the most dangerous animals in North America. A single blow from one of its mighty paws can break the neck or back of a moose.

Silver-Tipped Fur

This intelligent bear gets its name because its thick brown fur is tipped with silver-white, making it look grizzled. It needs a large territory in which to live and hunt, and is currently under threat from habitat loss due to human practices such as construction, logging, and mining.

Grizzlies will fight each other over food and territory.

GRIZZLY BEARS

URSUS ARCTOS HORRIBILIS

Habitat: Woodlands, forests, meadows; North America
Length: 2 m (6.5 ft)
Weight: Males up to 360 kg (790 lb); females up to 180 kg (400 lb)
Diet: Plants, nuts, berries, and roots, large and small mammals, fish, carrion
Lifespan: Up to 25 years

Grizzlies have a fantastic sense of smell. Some scientists say a grizzly can smell carrion from 28 km (18 mi) away.

This large grizzly has plenty of fat stores to see it through winter.

Grizzly bears have long sharp front teeth that can be up to 7.5cm (3 in) long!

Stock Up For Winter

During the second half of the year, a grizzly may eat 36–40 kg (80–90 lb) of food every single day—that's the equivalent of around 300 hamburgers! It builds up a layer of extra fat to allow it to survive the winter, when it may eat nothing at all for months.

The bite of a grizzly is thought to be strong enough to crush a bowling ball!

DID YOU KNOW? The grizzly walks on the soles and toes of its feet—just like a human!

More About Grizzlies

Grizzlies are among the most aggressive bears in the world, and one of the most likely to attack humans.

Stay Back!

Grizzlies are at their most dangerous when they feel threatened, cornered, or are wounded. A female defending her cubs is also likely to be highly aggressive. However, few grizzlies will actively hunt humans.

A mother bear teaches her cubs how to find food.

Hunting Techniques

Grizzlies use different fishing methods, learning their technique from their mother. Some stand still in the water and wait for a fish to jump out. Then they catch it in their jaws. Others use their paws to swat the fish out of the water and onto the shore.

DID YOU KNOW? Female grizzly bears will give birth to between one and four cubs at a time. The cubs are only 20–30 cm (8–12 in) long at birth.

The food that grizzlies like best is fish.

Like most bears, grizzlies live and hunt alone. However, once a year, during the summer, when the streams fill with salmon, grizzlies come together to fish.

Some grizzlies will swim underwater to find salmon, or stun the fish by flopping on top of them!

Kodiak Bears

Kodiaks do not have territories that they defend, but they do stay in the same areas each year.

The kodiak bear shares with the polar bear the status of world's largest land predator. Standing 3 m (10 ft) tall on its hind legs, this enormous beast is as tall as the high diving board at many swimming pools.

At Home in Alaska

The kodiak bear is a type of brown bear. It is found on the islands of the Kodiak Archipelago in Alaska. This is a salmon spawning ground, offering the kodiaks plenty of food.

Two kodiaks enjoy a play fight.

KODIAK BEARS

URSUS ARCTOS MIDDENDORFFI

Habitat: Forests and mountains; Southwest Alaska, North America
Length: Up to 3 m (10 ft)
Weight: Up to 680 kg (1,500 lb)
Diet: Grasses, plants, berries, roots, carrion, and salmon
Lifespan: Up to 25 years

Clever Creatures

The kodiak diet of high-protein, fatty salmon is the main reason for their huge size.

Kodiaks are not just big, they're also bright, with an intelligence estimated at somewhere between that of a dog and an ape. They have developed a complex language of noises and body movements and have recognizable personalities.

A kodiak chomps a breakfast treat.

Kodiaks have much better eyesight and hearing than the average bear.

A kodiak bear's claws are a mighty 12 cm (5 in) long.

DID YOU KNOW? The oldest kodiak bear ever found in the wild was 34 years old.

American Black Bears

The American black bear lives in the mountainous or heavily wooded areas of Canada, the United States, and Mexico. They are called black bears, but in fact their fur can be black, brown, silver-blue, and occasionally, even white!

Black bears will sometimes climb up trees to bald eagle nests. They eat the eggs or chicks.

Curved Claws

Black bears have small eyes, a long nose, round ears, and a short tail. Their feet have strong, very curved claws for climbing and digging.

Living Alone

Black bears spend most of their lives alone, unless they are females with cubs. Females give birth during winter hibernation, usually to two cubs.

Black bear cubs stay with their mother until they are about two years old. After that, they go off to live alone.

Black bears are able to climb trees with ease due to their short but strong claws!

Black bears often have a distinctive brown snout.

Even though black bears prefer forested areas, they also spend time near rivers. They will take to the water to find fish to eat!

Black bears are the smallest but most common type of bear found in the US.

AMERICAN BLACK BEARS

URSUS AMERICANUS

Habitat: Forests and mountainous areas; North America
Length: 1.3 to 1.9 m (4.3 to 6.2 ft)
Weight: males 270 kg (600 lb), females 90 kg (200 lb)
Diet: Plants, roots, grasses, berries, fish, and insects, as well as deer, moose, and livestock
Lifespan: Up to 25 years

DID YOU KNOW? A female black bear called Winnipeg, who lived in London Zoo from 1915 to 1934, was the inspiration for *Winnie the Pooh*.

More About American Black Bears

Black bears mostly eat nuts, fruits, and young leaves, but they also like to hunt. They prey on young deer, elk, and moose. Occasionally they might ambush a passing adult moose. They kill by biting the neck and shoulders or by using their paws to break the neck or back.

Less Aggressive

Black bears are not as aggressive as brown bears. They rarely attack humans, unless they are very hungry. Usually they will make mock charges, bare their teeth, and growl.

Black bears are good swimmers, which helps them catch fish.

Unlike brown bears, black bears do not have a shoulder hump.

Scavenge and Steal

Black bears have been known to scavenge carcasses from cougars and wolverines. They sometimes even steal deer from human hunters. Occasionally they prey on domestic livestock, such as sheep, goats, calves, and pigs.

Black bears have discovered that stealing human food is often easier than hunting.

Like their brown bear cousins, black bears are good at fishing.

Black bears eat up to 20 kg (45 lb) a day before hibernation.

DID YOU KNOW? Black bears have territories, but they usually do not defend them from other bears unless food is scarce.

Polar Bears

The polar bear is a powerful, skilled, and patient hunter that roams the coastal regions of the Arctic. Unlike other bears, it eats almost only meat. Its main prey are ringed and bearded seals, young walruses, and the occasional beluga whale.

At Home in the Cold

Polar bears are perfectly suited to their chilly environment. A four-inch layer of blubber and thick fur protects them from the cold. Their hollow outer hairs and black skin trap the sun's heat. Even their feet are adapted for the ice. In between their toes are long hairs that help create friction to stop them slipping.

Polar bears travel up to 14,500 km (9,000 mi) a year in search of food.

Powerful Paddlers

Polar bears have a number of advantages in the water. Their body fat gives them buoyancy and their broad forepaws, with webbed toes, help make swimming easy.

Polar bears can dive to a depth of 3 m (10 ft) or more!

DID YOU KNOW? Polar bear fur isn't actually white—it is completely transparent! Under their fur, their skin is black.

Polar bears will feast on carrion if they come across it while hunting.

Polar bears have large, sharp teeth, which they use to catch, kill and eat their prey.

Polar bears are the best swimmers in the bear family. They can swim for hours at a time, covering large distances.

POLAR BEARS

URSUS MARITIMUS

Habitat: Sea ice; Arctic Ocean
Length: Males 2.6 m (8.5 ft), females 1.3 m (4.25 ft)
Weight: Males up to 400–600 kg (880–1300 lb), females up to 150–250 kg (330–550 lb)
Diet: Seals, walrus, whales, carrion
Lifespan: Up to 30 years, but the average is 15–18

More About Polar Bears

Polar bears are stealth hunters. Their victims rarely know what is happening until the attack is under way.

Ambush Attack

Polar bears often ambush seals at their breathing holes. When the seal surfaces for air, the polar bear quickly seizes it.

Polar bear cubs learn to hunt by watching their mother.

Blood marks in the snow show where a polar bear has caught a seal. Polar bears are strong enough to crush seal skulls with their teeth.

Most often, polar bears give birth to two cubs at one time.

DID YOU KNOW? Polar bears have even been known to kill beluga whales—which are more than twice their weight!—by swiping at them at breathing holes.

A polar bear uses its great sense of smell to seek out its prey.

Seal Snacks!

Sometimes a polar bear might spot a seal on an ice floe. The bear creeps to within 12 m (40 ft) of the seal, then suddenly charges forward to attack.

Polar bears sometimes find seals' birthing dens beneath the ice. The bear rears onto its hind legs, then drops onto all fours, using its weight to smash through the ice and reach the baby seals.

Polar bears must kill at least 50 seals annually to survive.

Asiatic Black Bears

Asiatic black bears inhabit the mountain forests of South and East Asia. They are also known as moon bears because of the pale, crescent-shaped marking on their chest.

Asiatic black bears are loners. They can be aggressive, but generally prefer to avoid conflict.

Avoid the Cold

Asiatic black bears prefer warm weather. In Russia and northern China, bears hibernate when it gets cold. Farther south, bears migrate to warmer areas for the winter.

In the summer months, Asiatic black bears often build "nests" in trees. They sleep in them during the day and come down to feed at night.

ASIATIC BLACK BEARS

URSUS THIBETANUS

Habitat: Thickly forested mountain areas; East Asia
Length: 1.9 m (6.2 ft)
Weight: 40–200 kg (90–440 lb)
Diet: Fruit, nuts, leaves, cows, sheep, goats, and wild boar
Lifespan: About 25 years

These bears can be fierce. Even tigers have occasionally had their kills stolen by Asiatic black bears.

Top Predator

Asiatic black bears prey on mammals such as wild boar, water buffalo, sheep, and mountain goats. They kill them with powerful blows to the neck or back. However, Asiatic black bears mostly eat fruit, plants, eggs, insects, carrion, and food crops grown by humans.

Thanks to their strong, curved claws, Asiatic black bears are accomplished tree climbers.

DID YOU KNOW? Asiatic bears have between one and four cubs. The cubs stay with their mother for around two years.

Big Cats

Don't be fooled by the charm of a pet cat. Although small, it is a ferocious predator. Wild cats are even more formidable, perfectly adapted for catching and killing enough prey to feed themselves and their young.

All Over the World

All big cats are carnivores—they eat only meat. They are found in the Americas, Africa, Asia, and Europe, from cold mountaintops to the sweltering savanna.

These animals are apex predators, at the top of their food chain. Very few creatures will take on an adult lion or tiger. They have an important ecological role to play, helping with population control of their prey animals.

Tigers are the largest of the big cats and are found in Asia.

A lion's jaw can open to 28 cm (11 in) wide—now that's a huge bite!

Most big cats, like their smaller relatives, can climb trees. This is a cougar, or mountain lion.

Lions have a noble appearance and are sometimes called "kings of the jungle." They actually live in the African savanna.

Hunting Methods

Big cats are superb hunter-killers. They have keen eyesight, including night vision, and highly sensitive hearing. Their speed in the chase, sharp teeth and claws, and powerful jaws give them huge advantages when hunting for prey.

Male lions are much larger than the females.

DID YOU KNOW? Big cats, like pet cats, have a very rough tongue. It is covered with sharp points called papillae, which help to scrape meat off bones.

Lions

The lion is a large, powerful predator that lives in the grasslands of sub-Saharan Africa and Asia. Among the big cats, it is second only in size to the tiger.

Living Together

Unlike other big cats, which tend to be solitary, lions live in groups called prides. There can be up to 40 lions in a pride, most of which are females, called lionesses. Together, prides defend a territory that can be as large as 500 km² (200 sq miles).

Individual lions will sometimes break away from the pride for a few days at time to hunt for food or to find water. When they return, they greet each other by rubbing their heads together.

Females are smaller than the males. They look after the young, called cubs, and hunt for the pride.

While male lions are fast, females are even faster. These powerful creatures can run up to 80 km/h (50 mph) in short bursts.

An adult male lion fights a younger male. Incoming males often kill the cubs of those they have driven out, to give their own, future offspring a better chance of survival.

Fight to the Top

When it reaches maturity, around three years old, a male lion will leave its original pride. It will then fight the male of another pride to try to take its place. Older or injured male lions are vulnerable to attack by younger incoming males. If the new male lion is successful, it will mate with the females of the pride.

DID YOU KNOW? Lion cubs have spots on their skin to help camouflage them. The spots fade as the cubs grow older.

While the females hunt, male lions defend the pride and its territories.

Male lions are famous for their manes. In clashes with other animals, the mane makes the lion look bigger.

Big cats are famous for their roar. When they breathe out, the walls of the cat's larynx (voice box) vibrate, producing a deep, loud, rumbling sound.

AFRICAN LION

PANTHERA LEO

Habitat: Grasslands; sub-Saharan Africa
Length: Males up to 3 m (10 ft); females up to 1.7 m (5.7 ft)
Weight: Males 190 kg (420 lb); females 130 kg (280 lb)
Diet: Usually medium-size mammals
Lifespan: Males 12 years; females 15 years

How Lions Hunt

Most of the hunting is done by female lions. They can run very fast, but only in short bursts.

Power in Numbers

The lionesses hunt as a team, splitting into two groups. The larger group chases the prey—usually a herd of grazing animals—toward a smaller group lying in wait. When the herd are no more than 30 m (100 ft) away, the smaller group chases down their selected victim.

Lions prey on animals as small as rodents and as large as young elephants. Occasionally, lone male lions have been known to hunt humans. This usually happens because they are too injured or sick to hunt their usual prey.

The attack is swift and brutal. They leap onto the prey and sink their claws into its hindquarters, bringing it down, and then deliver a killer bite to its head or neck.

Lions prey mostly on zebra, wildebeest, and antelope, although they sometimes hunt buffalo, hippo, and giraffe.

ASIATIC LION

PANTHERA LEO PERSICA

Habitat: Grasslands, forests; Gir National Park, India
Length: Males up to 2.9 m (9.5 ft); females up to 1.7 m (5.7 ft)
Weight: Males up to 190 kg (420 lb); females up to 120 kg (265 lb)
Diet: Usually medium-size mammals
Lifespan: Males 16; females 17–18 years

First, a lioness stalks its warthog prey. Then, when it is close enough to strike, it attacks.

Time to Eat

A powerful lioness with her latest victim, a warthog. After a hunt, the males are the first to eat, followed by the females, and finally the cubs.

Typically, lions gorge on the fresh meat of a kill until they are full. They then hunt again a few days later, when they are hungry.

Lions do most of their hunting at night. Their eyes are six times more sensitive to light than human eyes, so they can see very well in the dark.

Lionesses are stealthy hunters, often taking their prey, such as this buffalo, by surprise.

DID YOU KNOW? Nearly all lions live in Africa, with the exception of a few hundred Asiatic lions that are found in India's Gir Forest.

Tigers

The tiger is the biggest of all the big cats and there are several subspecies. The biggest, the Amur tiger, can reach a total length of 3 m (10 ft), while the smallest, the Sumatran, averages just 2 m (6.5 ft).

Clever Camouflage

Tigers are among the most recognizable of the big cats. Their reddish orange fur and dark stripes provide ideal camouflage in the dense tropical forests of eastern and southern Asia where they live.

The pattern of stripes is unique to each tiger, like fingerprints on humans.

The Bengal tiger is the most numerous of all the tiger species and is the national animal of Bangladesh.

TIGER

PANTHERA TIGRIS

Habitat: Rain forests, grasslands, savannas; Asia
Length: Males 1.9–3.3 m (6.5–11 ft), females 1.8–2.5 m (6–8.5 ft)
Weight: Males up to 300 kg (660 lb), females up to 160 kg (360 lb)
Diet: Mostly mammals such as deer, antelope, and buffalo
Lifespan: 15–20 years

Water Lover

Tigers are unusual among big cats in their love of water, and they can often be seen cooling off in ponds, lakes, and rivers. They have been known to swim almost 5 km (3 mi) in a day.

Tigers usually live and hunt alone, defending their territory against other tigers. A tiger's territory can be 18–90 km² (7–35 sq mi), depending on how much available prey there is.

Two tigers play fight in the water.

Habitat loss and hunting has greatly reduced numbers of tigers in the wild.

Tigers can reach speeds of up to 48-64 km/h (30–40 mph) in short bursts.

DID YOU KNOW? If you were to shave a tiger, you would find the same pattern on its skin!

How Tigers Hunt

Tigers mainly hunt at night. They target larger animals, such as wild boar, buffalo, and deer, but will hunt smaller animals such as monkeys, peafowl, hares, and fish when the others aren't available.

Tigers have to be very patient, as only around one in ten hunts ends in a kill.

Surprise Attack

The tiger hunts alone, but has been known to share its kills with others in its family group. It ambushes its prey by hiding in thick vegetation and then leaping out when its victim strays near.

Powerful Predator

The tiger grabs its prey with its forelimbs, using its size and strength to push the prey off balance. It then delivers a deadly bite to the throat. It keeps its jaws clamped to the throat until the victim dies of suffocation.

Because of its use of strength, speed, and surprise, the tiger is able to overpower prey much larger than itself, including the water buffalo, which can weigh over a ton—six times heavier than its attacker.

Tigers will scent-mark their territory to warn other tigers to stay away.

DID YOU KNOW? Tiger cubs are born blind, gaining their sight after one or two weeks.

Amur tigers live only in the far east of Russia and China. They have thicker fur than other tigers to protect them from the cold.

A tiger can cover up to 10 m (33 ft) in a single leap.

A tiger stalks a deer. It tries to get as close as possible to its prey before making the final charge.

Leopards

Leopards are smaller than lions and tigers, with relatively short legs and a long body. Like jaguars, their fur is covered in rosettes, but leopard rosettes are smaller than jaguar ones, and have no internal spots.

The leopard is larger and stronger than the cheetah, but smaller and more lightly built than the jaguar.

Golden Fur

The most adaptable of the big cats, leopards are found in desert, open grassland, forest, and mountain regions. The fur varies from cream to deep gold, depending on where they live, to give them the best chance of blending into their surroundings.

Leopards and crocodiles are the only known predators of gorillas.

Sometimes they clash with other leopards when defending their territories, which can range from 15–77 sq km (6–30 sq mi) in size.

LEOPARD

PANTHERA PARDUS

Habitat: Savannas, grasslands, deserts; Sub-Saharan Africa, Southeast Asia
Length: Up to 1.5 m (5 ft)
Weight: 21–72 kg (46–158 lb)
Diet: Small antelope, warthogs, birds, hares, and rabbits
Lifespan: Around 12 years

Up in the Trees

Leopards are solitary creatures, and are generally active at night. They spend their days resting on tree branches or in caves. Their powerful shoulder muscles make them excellent tree climbers. They are also good swimmers.

Leopards' tree climbing skills can come in handy when they face a threat from larger relatives such as lions and tigers.

A leopard's tail is almost as long as its body. Its tail gives it great balance.

DID YOU KNOW? Some forest leopards are born with black fur and are known as panthers. Black-furred jaguars are also called panthers.

How Leopards Hunt

Leopards are agile, stealthy predators, stalking their prey silently before pouncing with lethal suddenness. They clamp their powerful jaws around their victim's throat, holding on until the animal dies of suffocation.

Before it strikes, a leopard will stalk its prey to get as close as possible to its target.

Night and Day

In savanna and desert areas, leopards mostly hunt at night, while forest leopards often hunt during the day, using their natural camouflage to conceal themselves in the dense vegetation.

Leopards will scratch trees and spray urine to mark their territory, like other big cats.

A leopard's teeth are up to 5 cm (2 in) long, and are used to bite and pierce.

Not Fussy!

Leopards will eat virtually any animal they can catch, including insects, rodents, reptiles, and fish. However, they mainly target smaller antelope and deer, such as impalas, gazelles, chitals, and duikers.

Leopards living near human settlements have been known to attack domestic livestock such as goats and pigs, and occasionally even people.

DID YOU KNOW? Scientists studying leopards in parts of Africa have counted at least 90 different species eaten by the big cats.

Leopards communicate using calls, such as growling, when they are angered.

Once it has its prey within reach, it charges at full speed before pouncing.

Leopards are the only big cats to hide their prey in trees. They can drag prey three times their own weight (including full-grown antelopes or even young giraffes) high into treetops.

Jaguars

The jaguar is the largest big cat in the Western Hemisphere and the third largest overall. It inhabits the forests and grassy plains of Central and South America.

The jaguar looks similar to the leopard, but it is larger and more powerfully built, with a rounder head.

Excellent Swimmers

Like tigers, jaguars love swimming and are often found near water. They are also very good tree climbers. Once they have matured, around the age of four, jaguars spend much of their lives alone, meeting others only when it is time to reproduce.

Jaguars generally avoid each other, but sometimes they clash if there is a dispute over territory.

JAGUAR

PANTHERA ONCA

Habitat: Forests and wetlands; South and Central America
Length: Up to 1.8 m (6 ft)
Weight: Up to 96 kg (211 lb)
Diet: Deer, capybaras, monkeys, caiman, lizards, fish, birds
Lifespan: Up to 15 years

DID YOU KNOW? The jaguar's roar sounds similar to a repeated cough. It is also known to make grunting and mewing sounds.

Black Panthers

Like leopards, jaguars are sometimes born with black fur and are known as panthers. Although they appear perfectly black, their spots are visible on close inspection.

Black panthers are sometimes called ghosts of the forest, as they are so hard to spot.

A jaguar's rosettes are bigger than a leopard's and have small spots in the middle.

The most active times of day for a jaguar are the hours of dawn and dusk.

How Jaguars Hunt

The jaguar hunts alone, stalking and ambushing its prey. It prefers the larger mammals and reptiles of the forest and the grassland plains, such as deer, tapirs, capybaras, and caimans, but will make do with foxes, frogs, and rodents. It may also hunt monkeys and sloths in the lower branches of trees.

At Home in the Water

Jaguars sometimes leap into rivers and attack caimans, turtles, fish, and even anacondas.

Creeping Closer

Walking slowly down forest paths, the jaguar listens for its prey. When the target is sighted, it creeps closer, finding a concealed position to the rear of the animal, before pouncing. It kills its prey with a powerful bite to the skull between the ears, piercing the brain.

DID YOU KNOW? About half of the world's wild population of jaguars live in Brazil.

Its muscular jaws and long, sharp canines enable the jaguar to bite through the shells of turtles or the thick skin of a caiman.

Jaguars are confident hunters in water environments, often crossing rivers to hunt.

The legs of a jaguar are relatively short but very powerful.

The jaguar can bite down with well over a ton of force. For its size, its bite is stronger than that of a tiger or a lion.

Cougars

The cougar is found right across the Western Hemisphere, from Canada to Chile. An extremely adaptable animal, it thrives in a range of habitats, including mountains, forests, prairies, and deserts.

Many Names

Perhaps because of this, the cougar has a remarkable number of names, known in different places as puma, mountain lion, red tiger, deercat, mountain devil, Mexican lion, mountain screamer, catamount, and sneak cat.

Cougars are lean, agile creatures with a round head and erect ears. They are the only big cat without fur markings, apart from the African lion.

Unlike other big cats, the cougar cannot roar, but it can make other surprising sounds, such as chirps, peeps, whistles, and even screams.

COUGAR

PUMA CONCOLOR

Habitat: Forests, mountains, deserts; North and South America
Weight: Males 90 kg (200 lb), females 54 kg (120 lb)
Length: Males 2.4 m (7.8 ft), females 2 m (6.5 ft)
Diet: Mammals such as deer, coyote, and hares
Lifespan: Up to 13 years

A cougar's strong, muscular body is brown on its back and white underneath.

After a cougar has finished with its prey, it may cover it with sticks and leaves—and come back to eat more later.

Deadly Leap

The cougar is a stalk-and-ambush predator, armed with long, sharp canines and retractable claws. It can kill an elk by jumping on its back and pulling with its forelegs to break its neck. It will often bury its kill to conceal it from scavengers.

DID YOU KNOW? Cougars can make leaps of up to 6 m (20 ft) in pursuit of prey.

55

Cheetahs

The cheetah is built for one purpose—speed. It lives in the flat, treeless, grassy plains of sub-Saharan Africa where swiftness in the chase is a huge advantage for a predator.

The cheetah has a top speed around 114 km/h (71 mph), making it the world's fastest land animal!

Built For Speed

This big cat has a streamlined body, strong, thin legs, and light bones. Its body features are perfect for fast acceleration in short burts.

The cheetah also boasts hard-padded paws and semi-retractable claws for an efficient grip, and its large nostrils and lungs help it take in extra oxygen in the closing stages of a sprint.

A Deadly Chase

The cheetah has very good eyesight, so prefers to hunt during the day. It follows herds of gazelle or impala, looking for old, young or injured animals. Once it has found its target, it will creep as close as possible before giving chase. Full sprints last only around 20 seconds.

DID YOU KNOW? The cheetah can easily be identified by the black rings on its tail and the "tear marks" on its face.

The cheetah's flexible spine works like a spring for its back legs, giving it extra reach for each stride.

Cheetahs will form small groups, often made up of brothers from the same litter.

With its exceptional speed, the cheetah usually manages to outrun its victims. After bringing down the animal, the cheetah clamps its powerful jaws around its windpipe, suffocating it.

CHEETAH

ACINONYX JUBATUS

Habitat: Savannas, grasslands, deserts; Sub-Saharan Africa plus small populations in both North Africa and Iran
Weight: Up to 72 kg (158 lb)
Length: Up to 1.5 m (5 ft)
Diet: Mostly small antelope, also rabbits, warthogs, and birds
Lifespan: Around 12 years

Snow Leopards

The snow leopard is a solitary cat inhabiting the mountains of Central Asia. Its thick, woolly fur keeps it warm in its chilly environment. The fur is white, yellowish, or a smoky brown. It is covered in dark rosettes, providing it with excellent camouflage on rocky mountainsides.

Mountain Dweller

The cat's short forelimbs and long hind legs give it agility on steep, rugged mountain slopes. Its tail gives it balance, and its large paws help it to walk on snow. All these attributes help the snow leopard when hunting mountain sheep and goats—its prey of choice.

Snow leopards are shy, elusive cats, rarely seen in the wild.

A mother snow leopard with her cubs. Snow leopards spend most of their life alone, and when the cubs mature, at the age of 18 to 22 months, they will move far away, seeking new hunting grounds.

A snow leopard will wrap itself up in its long thick tail to protect itself from the cold.

These beautiful big cats can live as high up as 5,000 m (16,400 ft).

Huge Meals

The snow leopard hunts at dawn and dusk. It kills large animals roughly twice a month. These can take several days to devour.

When sheep or goats aren't available, the snow leopard will eat smaller animals such as marmots, hares, rodents, and birds. Unusually for a big cat, it will sometimes even eat plants.

The snow leopard has extremely powerful hind legs.

SNOW LEOPARD

PANTHERA UNCIA

Habitat: Mountain areas; Central Asia
Length: 2.1 m (7 ft)
Weight: 25–55 kg (55–120 lb)
Diet: Sheep, goats, small mammals, and birds
Lifespan: Up to 18 years

DID YOU KNOW? Snow leopards can leap distances more than 9 m (30 ft)—that's five times its body length!

Lynxes

The lynx inhabits the remote forests and snowy wastes of northern Europe, Asia, and North America. It has soft, thick fur to keep it warm during the harsh winters, and big feet to help it walk through deep snow.

Up High

A skilled climber, the lynx likes to spend much of its time in the branches of trees, waiting for prey such as mammals or non-flying birds to pass beneath it.

Small but Deadly

The lynx hunts by stalking and ambushing its prey. It has acute hearing and vision, sensitive whiskers, and quick reflexes to help it hunt.

Larger Eurasian lynxes have enough strength and agility to catch and kill a reindeer or caribou, despite being no bigger than an average-sized dog.

The tufts of black hair on the lynx's ears direct sound into its ears and enhance its hearing.

The thick fur of a lynx keeps it warm throughout the cold winter months.

DID YOU KNOW? The lynx has excellent eyesight. It is said to be able to spot a mouse from 75 m (250 ft) away.

Canadian lynx are so dependent on the snowshoe hare as prey that when their numbers decline, about once every ten years, there is a corresponding fall in the lynx population.

The fur of a lynx is patterned with lots of dark spots.

Lynx are often described as secretive animals. They are hard to spot in the wild!

LYNX

LYNX CANADENSIS

Habitat: Dense woodland, mountain ranges; Europe, Asia, and North America
Length: 90–130 cm (37–52 in)
Weight: 9 kg (20 lb)
Diet: Snowshoe hare, mice, squirrels, and birds
Lifespan: Up to 15 years

Crocodiles and Alligators

The crocodilian animal group includes crocodiles, alligators, gharials, and caimans. These creatures spend much of their day basking in the sun to help them stay warm. They are all cold-blooded, which means they can't regulate their body temperature.

In the Water

Although crocodilians move with reasonable agility on land, they are far more at home in the water. They splay their limbs to steer with and to keep themselves afloat, and use their tail for thrust.

Crocodilians are superb swimmers. They sweep their powerful tail from side to side to propel themselves through the water.

The claws on a crocodilian's front feet are useful for dragging itself up onto shore.

CUBAN CROCODILE

CROCODYLUS RHOMBIFER

Habitat: Freshwater swamps; Cuba
Length: Up to 3.5 m (11.5 ft)
Weight: Typically up to 80 kg (180 lb)
Diet: Fish, turtles, and small mammals
Lifespan: Up to 75 years

Unique Run

On land, crocodilians usually move in lizard fashion, crawling along with their belly close to the ground and legs splayed out to the sides. But when necessary, they are capable of moving in ways unique among reptiles, walking and even running with their legs beneath their body—almost like a mammal.

This crocodile is doing the "high walk," lifting its entire body and most of its tail off the ground.

This Cuban crocodile is covered in rough scales called scutes. Even though it has a very thick skin, it can still move easily underwater.

DID YOU KNOW? The Nile crocodile can travel up to 9 km (5.5 miles) in one night.

63

American Crocodiles

The American crocodile is one of the bigger crocodilians, and the largest in the Americas. It is found mainly in Central America, but also appears in parts of South America and Florida.

Broad Snout

The American crocodile has a wide snout, enabling it to eat a wider variety of prey. Its snout gets broader as the animal ages.

The American croc dwells in warm, shallow waters such as mangrove swamps, coves, creeks, coastal lagoons, river mouths, and even the open sea.

Unlike the alligator, crocodiles can't stand the cold, which is why it sticks to tropical areas.

AMERICAN CROCODILE

CROCODYLUS ACUTUS

Habitat: Coastal, estuarine, freshwater habitats; Southern US, Central America, South America
Length: Average 4 m (13 ft) but up to 6 m (20 ft) long
Weight: Male up to 500 kg (1,100 lb), females around 170 kg (370 lb)
Diet: Fish, crustaceans, reptiles, amphibians, mammals
Lifespan: Up to 70 years

Nocturnal Predator

American crocodiles hunt mostly at night. They eat fish, turtles, and crabs, but also birds, insects, mammals, snails, frogs, and occasionally carrion. They are less aggressive than Nile and Australian crocodiles, but have been known to attack humans.

Crocodiles have extremely strong, sharp teeth that are replaced as they wear out.

Both alligators and crocodiles are covered in thick, plated scales to protect their body.

An American crocodile displays its 66 teeth. Note the prominent fourth tooth on the lower jaw, which distinguishes crocodiles from their alligator cousins.

DID YOU KNOW? American crocodiles sometimes regurgitate bits of food to use as bait to attract fish.

Nile Crocodiles

Africa's largest crocodilian, the Nile crocodile is a ferocious predator with a reputation for attacking people. It is found in lakes, rivers, swamps, and brackish (slightly salty) water across sub-Saharan Africa.

Deadly Hunter

Nile crocodiles are voracious animals and will eat almost anything that moves. They often hunt on their own, but will sometimes gather into a group. They form a barrier in the water to trap fish, which they then eat.

Nile crocodiles lay their eggs in the riverbank. They are very protective of their nests, guarding them fiercely until their eggs hatch.

The thick skin of a Nile crocodile makes it hard for would-be attackers to cause injury.

Fierce Competition

Nile crocodiles often compete with other African predators, especially big cats. When food is scarce, they have been known to prey on each other. The animal that takes the first bite is in with a good chance of winning the fight.

Lions and crocodiles hunt similar prey, which can result in a stand-off.

DID YOU KNOW? The Nile crocodile can eat up to half its own weight during one meal!

66

NILE CROCODILE

CROCODYLUS NILOTICUS

Habitat: Rivers, lakes, mangrove swamps, and streams; sub-saharan Africa and Madagascar
Length: Up to 6 m (19.6 ft)
Weight: 225-750 kg (500-1,650 lbs)
Diet: Mostly fish, but also zebras, small hippos, antelopes, porcupines, birds, and even other crocodiles
Lifespan: 40-60 years

Nile crocodiles were hunted to near extinction, yet their numbers have steadily recovered over the last 80 years or so.

A Nile crocodile surges out of the Mara river to attack wildebeest.

Freshwater Crocodiles

The freshwater crocodile is a small crocodilian, found in the lakes, billabongs, swamps, rivers, and creeks of northern Australia. Despite its name, it can tolerate salt water, but is kept away from coastal areas by its larger, more aggressive cousin, the saltwater crocodile.

At Home in the Water

Freshwater crocodiles live in areas that commonly flood. After heavy rainfall, the waterways become linked, meaning the crocodiles can move around easily. When the water levels drop and return to normal, the crocodiles must stick to deeper bodies of water to avoid getting stranded.

The freshwater crocodile's skin has stripes of very dark patches across its sides.

Freshies have strong legs and clawed, webbed hind feet, which help make them agile swimmers.

DID YOU KNOW? When food is scarce, freshwater crocodiles have been known to turn cannibal and eat the hatchlings of their own species.

A Powerful Snap

"Freshies" mostly feed on animals that stray too close to the water's edge. Like all crocodilians, they are ambush predators. This means that they can lie motionless in the water for hours on end. Then, with a lightning-quick snap of the head, the fish or frog they've been watching finds itself helpless in their jaws.

It has a long, narrow snout and a mouth lined with 68–72 sharp teeth.

This croc is well adapted for catching insects and small, aquatic prey.

FRESHWATER CROCODILE

CROCODYLUS JOHNSTONI

Habitat: Lakes, billabongs, swamps, rivers, and creeks; Northern Australia
Length: Males 2–3 m (6.6–10 ft); females 1.8–3 m (6–6.6 ft)
Weight: Males 70 kg (150 lb), females 40 kg (88 lb)
Diet: Insects, crustaceans, fish, amphibians, reptiles, bats, and small mammals
Lifespan: 45 years in the wild; up to 80 years in captivity

Saltwater Crocodiles

The saltwater crocodile is the largest reptile on the planet, and—some would say—the most dangerous to humans. This big, aggressive beast is a supreme predator, able and willing to attack anything made of flesh and bone that comes within range.

Super Swimmers

These crocs live in brackish and freshwater areas of eastern India, Southeast Asia, and northern Australia. They are commonly found in rivers, swamps, and estuaries, but have also been sighted far out to sea.

Saltwater crocs are big and strong enough to drag large mammals into the water and kill them with a single bite to the skull.

Expert hunters

Young salties feed on insects, amphibians, crustaceans, small reptiles, and fish. But the more they grow, the bigger their prey. Large adults will tackle any creature, up to and including cows, horses, and water buffalo.

Saltwater crocodiles snatch fish from the water and swallow them whole.

Saltwater crocodiles are also known as "Salties."

DID YOU KNOW? Saltwater crocodiles can open their mouth under water. There is a valve at the back of their throat to stop water going down.

Using their powerful tail to propel them, salties can swim very fast in short bursts.

Male saltwater crocodiles are typically much larger than the females.

SALTWATER CROCODILE

CROCODYLUS POROSUS

Habitat: Freshwater swamps, rivers, and estuaries, Southeast Asia, India, and Australia
Length: Males average 4-5 m (13-16 ft), and females 2.5-3.3 m (8-11 ft)
Weight: Average 450 kg (1,000 lb)
Diet: Fish, mammals, and birds
Lifespan: 70 years

Alligators

Alligators come from a different branch of the crocodilian family from crocodiles. Like crocodiles, alligators have strong jaws that enable them to eat hard-shelled creatures such as turtles, which form an important part of their diet.

Top Tail

An alligator propels itself through water with a powerful tail that is almost half its length. It also uses its tail to make gator holes, which are pools of water to wallow in. An alligator's tail stores fat that can help it survive when there is less food to hunt.

An alligator's skin is extremely sensitive. It can sense even very small vibrations made by nearby prey or would-be attackers.

Two Types

There are two types of alligator—the American, which lives in the south-eastern United States, and the Chinese, dwelling in the Yangtze River valley. Both live in marshes, ponds, and rivers. They are solitary animals, generally timid toward humans, but can attack if provoked.

Like all crocodilians, alligators are ambush predators that lie in wait for their prey before attacking.

DID YOU KNOW? The first alligator ancestors walked the Earth some 200 million years ago!

AMERICAN ALLIGATOR

ALLIGATOR MISSISSIPPIENSIS

Habitat: Marshes, swamps, rivers, and ponds; North America
Length: 3-4.5 m (10-15 ft)
Weight: 360 kg (800 lb)
Diet: Fish, turtles, and small mammals
Lifespan: Typically 50 years, but one specimen in a Latvian zoo lived more than 75 years

The alligator has a wider upper jaw than the crocodile, and the teeth of its lower jaw disappear when its mouth is closed.

American alligators were once on the brink of extinction, yet today their numbers are growing.

The alligator's sharp, conical teeth are used for catching prey or tearing off chunks of flesh, which they then swallow whole.

Gharials

The gharial, also known as the gavial, is instantly recognizable from its long, narrow snout. It has evolved this way because of its almost exclusive diet of small fish.

Fishy Diet

The gharial's slender snout—the narrowest of any crocodilian species—offers very little water resistance, enabling it to jerk its head sideways through the water at great speed, and snatch up fish in its jaws.

On land, the gharial is awkward—its short, stumpy legs are ill-adapted for walking. Yet in the water, it is a strong, graceful swimmer.

The gharial's many needle-sharp teeth are ideal for gripping onto wriggling, slippery fish.

Water Dweller

The gharial lives in deep, fast-flowing rivers in parts of northern India and Nepal, though it used to be far more widespread. The most aquatic of all crocodilians, it comes out of the water only to bask in the warm sun or to build a nest during the dry season.

Gharials have a strong, flattened tail and webbed hind feet.

DID YOU KNOW? Gharials swallow small rocks to crush the food in their stomach and to help them digest their meals!

Gharials have distinctive eyes that bulge from their head.

The gharial gets its name from the knob at the end of its nose, which resembles an Indian "ghara," or pot.

GHARIAL

GAVIALIS GANGETICUS

Habitat: Rivers; India and Nepal
Length: Average 3–4.5 m (11–15 ft)—although 6 m (20 ft) specimens have been found
Weight: 680–1,000 kg (1,500–2,200 lb)
Diet: Fish, turtles, and small mammals
Lifespan: 40–60 years in the wild

Caimans

The caiman belongs to the same branch of the crocodilian family as the alligator, and shares that creature's wide, short head and preference for fresh water. There are five species of caiman, all of which inhabit the wetland regions of Central and South America.

Crocodile Cousins

Like their crocodile cousins, caimans spend their days resting and basking. At night they are more active, choosing to hunt after dark.

While other crocodilians lay their eggs in holes, caimans build large mound nests. Once the females have laid their eggs, they guard them from potential predators until they have safely hatched.

The spectacled caiman is so named because the bony ridge between its eyes resembles a pair of spectacles.

Cuvier's dwarf caiman is the smallest of all crocodilians, reaching no more than 1.5 m (5 ft) long.

BLACK CAIMAN

MELANOSUCHUS NIGER

Habitat: Amazon basin; South America
Length: 4–5 m (13–16 ft)
Weight: Up to 300 kg (660 lbs)
Diet: Fish, other reptiles, and capybaras
Lifespan: 40 years

Biggest of All

The black caiman is the largest member of the alligator family. Males average 4 m (13 ft), with the largest recorded size at 5 m (16 ft). Like the American alligator, the black caiman has been known to attack humans and domestic livestock.

The black caiman's dark skin helps to absorb heat from the sun.

The shading of a caiman's skin can vary greatly from olive green to brown and black. This gives it great camouflage.

Caimans can be found in freshwater habitats from southern Mexico to northern Argentina.

DID YOU KNOW? Research has shown that caimans time their mating with the rainfall cycles and river levels in order to give their offspring the best chance of survival.

77

Sharks

Few creatures can induce fear like the sleek, deadly hunter of the ocean—the shark. Its speed, powerful jaws, and razor-sharp teeth combine to make it one of nature's most lethal hunters!

Swimming Machines

Sharks have a torpedo-shaped body and powerful tail that can propel them at speeds of 50 km/h (30 mph). They also have a superb sense of smell, and can scent blood in the water from far away. They possess additional senses to detect the tiny vibrations and deep sounds made by their prey.

Blue water, white death—the great white shark is quite possibly the scariest creature in the sea!

Scary Sight!

The ultimate shark movie cliché: a dorsal fin knifes through the water toward unsuspecting swimmers. In fact, it is rare for sharks to swim in this way, except in very shallow water.

DID YOU KNOW? Sharks are fish, and belong to the same family as rays and skates. Their skeletons are made of cartilage, not bone.

While some sharks can be extremely dangerous to humans, many kinds are peaceful creatures.

Sharks have been alive on Earth since before the dinosaurs!

Shark teeth are perfectly adapted for eating meat. This tooth, from a great white, has serrated edges—ideal for cutting through flesh and bone.

Most shark attacks on humans have been by great whites, bull sharks, and tiger sharks.

Great White Sharks

Legendary star of the movie *Jaws*, the great white is the most famous, and the most feared, of all sharks. Its black eyes, streamlined body, and terrifying teeth are, for many people, the stuff of nightmares.

The back of a great white is darker than its white belly. This camouflages it in deep water, enabling it to surprise its prey from below.

Great whites belong to a group of sharks called mackerel sharks.

Warm Bodies

Great whites are found in almost all the world's seas and oceans. Because they can keep their body temperature higher than the surrounding water, they can survive in very cold seas.

GREAT WHITE SHARK	
CARCHARODON CARCHARIAS	**Habitat:** Temperate coastal waters; Worldwide **Length:** Around 4.6 m (15 ft) **Weight:** 680–1800 kg (0.75–2 tons) **Diet:** Fish, rays, sharks, marine mammals **Lifespan:** Around 70 years

DID YOU KNOW? The biggest recorded great white was caught in Cuban waters in 1945. It was an incredible 6.4 m (21 ft) long!

Great whites are the largest of all predatory sharks. They swim from the ocean's surface down to the seafloor as they search for prey.

Great whites are responsible for the majority of recorded attacks on humans. This may be because they mistake surfers and divers for prey.

Spotting Prey

Unusually for sharks, great whites can raise their head above the water—useful for checking out seals basking on rocks.

More About Great Whites

Great white sharks eat seals, otters, seabirds, fish, dolphins, squid, turtles, and even other sharks. They are stealth hunters, who tend to surprise their prey by swimming at them fast from below.

Seal Snack

Small seals are struck in mid-body and often tossed clear out of the water, or else grabbed from the surface and pulled down. Large seals are bitten and left to bleed to death.

The great white cuts through the water at an incredible 40 km/h (24mph), many times faster than a human swimmer.

Shark skin has tiny overlapping scales that help reduce friction in the water.

A great white shark devours a seal near South Africa.

Great whites have about 3,000 teeth arranged in rows. When the front teeth get broken or worn, the next row of teeth moves forward to take their place.

Electric Senses

Like other sharks, great whites have an extra sense that enables them to detect the faint electrical pulses that animals emit when they move. A shark's electric sensors are found on its head and snout—they look like large pores and are called ampullae of Lorenzini. Great whites are so sensitive, they can detect a creature's heartbeat.

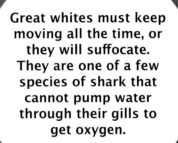

Great whites must keep moving all the time, or they will suffocate. They are one of a few species of shark that cannot pump water through their gills to get oxygen.

Tiger Sharks

As their name suggests, tiger sharks are fierce and aggressive predators. They are commonly found in the warm shallow waters of the tropics, but are equally happy in the ocean depths or murky river estuaries.

Night Hunter

Tiger sharks mostly hunt on their own, and are nocturnal, meaning they are most active at night. They swim quite slowly through the dark waters, which enables them to creep up on their prey without being spotted.

Tiger sharks have good night vision. A clear membrane covers their eyes when lunging at prey to protect the eyes from damage.

The tiger shark has rows of teeth. Like the great white, the teeth are constantly replaced throughout the shark's life.

Tiger sharks mostly live in shallow waters close to coasts.

This tiger shark is sneaking up on its seabird prey.

Rip and Tear

The tiger shark's serrated teeth are shorter than the teeth of the great white, and they point to the side. They are perfectly adapted to pierce, tear, and saw through the hard skin and shells of various prey.

Even though tiger sharks are deadly predators, they themselves may be hunted by killer whales.

TIGER SHARK

GALEOCERDO CUVIER

Habitat: Warm, tropical waters; Japan, China, Australia, Indonesia, Africa, India, North America, Central America, and South America
Length: 4.25 m (14 ft)
Weight: Up to 635 kg (1,400 lb)
Diet: Marine birds, marine mammals, turtles, bony fish, crustaceans, squid, skates, and rays
Lifespan: Around 12 years

DID YOU KNOW? The largest recorded tiger shark was a female caught in 1957. It was an incredible 7.3 m (24 ft) long!

More About Tiger Sharks

The tiger shark has a varied diet, including seabirds, sea snakes, seals, turtles, crustaceans, fish, squid, whale carcasses, and almost anything else it comes across.

A Strange Diet

Tiger sharks have been known to eat bottles, cans, alarm clocks, baseballs, boat cushions, hubcaps, raincoats, handbags, and shoes. Some unexpected animal parts have shown up in tiger shark stomachs too, including cow hooves, deer antlers, a crocodile's head, a horse's head, cats, pigs, and chickens!

Tiger sharks are the second largest predatory shark after the great white, and the fourth largest of all shark species.

Tiger sharks have been given the nickname "Garbage Can of the Sea" due to all the strange things they will eat!

Tiger sharks are a migratory species, swimming vast distances each year to find warmer waters.

DID YOU KNOW? In 1935, a tiger shark, introduced to an Australian aquarium, vomited up a human arm. The person the arm belonged to was identified by a tattoo.

As tiger sharks live in coastal waters, they are more likely to come into contact with humans. Their big appetite and aggressive nature can make them a danger to divers and swimmers.

Special Markings

Tiger sharks are so named because when they are young their skin is covered with tigerlike stripes. These fade as they mature.

The tiger shark has a wide mouth and a blunt nose. Its long fins give it lift as it moves through the water.

Bull Sharks

The bull shark is named for its short, stout body and fierce reputation. It is found in all the world's warmer seas and oceans from Australia to South America.

Bump and Bite

A bull shark has poor eyesight, and often swims in murky waters. It hunts by headbutting its prey to work out what it is, before sinking its teeth into it.

Bull sharks are agile swimmers. They can reach speeds of up to 40 km/h (25 mph)!

Dark, muddy water is an advantage for the shark, and its prey can't see it coming.

The bull shark's mouth is crammed with hundreds of sharp, pointed teeth.

BULL SHARK

CARCHARHINUS LEUCAS

Habitat: Coastal waters and rivers; Worldwide
Length: Males 2 m (7 ft), females 3.3 m (11 ft)
Weight: 90–230 kg (200–500 lb)
Diet: Fish, sharks, marine mammals such as dolphins, crustaceans, turtles, sea birds
Lifespan: Around 14 years

Fresh Water Swimmers

Alone among sharks, bulls can swim in both salt water and fresh water, and are often seen in rivers and lakes. In fact, bull sharks have been reported hundreds of miles up the Amazon and Mississippi rivers.

When in fresh water, bull sharks have been known to dine on antelopes, horses, hippos, cows, sloths, dogs, birds, and even rats!

Bull sharks can tolerate fresh water by reducing the amount of salt and urea in their bodies. They do this by peeing a lot—roughly 20 times as much as when they're in the ocean!

DID YOU KNOW? Bull sharks have the strongest bite force of any shark, even more powerful than a great white of the same size!

Lemon Sharks

The lemon shark gets its name from its yellowish brown skin. It frequents the warmer coastal waters of the Atlantic and Pacific, and is often seen in bays, docks, and river mouths.

Clever Camouflage

The shading of a lemon shark's skin gives it great camouflage against the sandy seabed as it searches for food. Groups of these sharks gather together twice a day—in the morning and evening—to feed.

Lemon sharks give birth to live young. As soon as they are born, the baby sharks hunt for themselves. They receive no parental care.

Lemon sharks have a particularly short, blunt snout.

This shark is accompanied by a remora. The fish travels along with the shark and removes parasites from its body.

Shark Nurseries

After a lemon shark is born, it heads towards the shallow waters found at mangrove swamps. Here, it finds other baby sharks in an area called a shark nursery. Together the young sharks learn hunting skills.

When a large quantity of food comes their way, these sharks can be provoked into a feeding frenzy.

LEMON SHARK

NEGAPRION BREVIROSTRIS

Habitat: Warm, shallow waters; Africa, North America, Central America, and South America
Length: Up to 3 m (10 ft)
Weight: 250 kg (550 lb)
Diet: Bony fish, rays, seabirds, and small sharks
Lifespan: 30 years

DID YOU KNOW? Lemon sharks have very poor eyesight. They make up for this with powerful sensors in their nose which can pick up the electrical pulses of their prey.

Blue Sharks

Blue sharks are superb long-distance swimmers, and have been known to swim thousands of miles in just a few months. They have been found off the coasts of every continent except Antarctica.

Metallic Blue

These beautiful sharks are named after the vibrant blue shade on the top of their body. They blend in perfectly with their open ocean surroundings from above, which lets them sneak up on their prey.

In a group of blue sharks, a hierarchy forms, like in a wolf pack.

The underside of a blue shark is white, which gives it camouflage from below.

Shark Pack

Blue sharks often travel and hunt in groups, which gives them their nickname, "Wolves of the Sea." They eat small fish, octopus, lobster, shrimp, and crab. Whale and porpoise meat have also been found in blue shark stomachs, but their ideal meal is squid.

BLUE SHARK

PRIONACE GLAUCA

Habitat: Deep and shallow waters; Worldwide
Length: 3 m (10 ft)
Weight: 100 kg (220 lb)
Diet: Squid, fish, octopus, and sometimes dead whales and dolphins
Lifespan: Up to 20 years

With its long snout and sleek, torpedo-shaped body, the blue shark can cut through the water at very high speeds, especially when chasing down prey.

When hunting, blue sharks rely on speed. They swim quickly through a group of squid with their jaws open, eating as many as they can.

A blue shark, off the coast of California, has found a shoal of fish to feast on!

DID YOU KNOW? The blue shark is the most widely dispersed shark on the planet. It is found in all the world's seas and oceans, from Scandinavia to the tip of South America.

Shortfin Mako Sharks

The shortfin mako takes the prize for fastest swimmer in the shark world. It can reach an astonishing 96 km/h (60 mph), over short bursts, and can jump up to 9 m (30 ft) into the air.

Super Speedy

Because of their super speed, shortfin makos can chase down some extremely fast prey, including tuna, swordfish, sailfish, and other sharks.

The shortfin mako's streamlined shape and frictionless scales help make it one of the fastest predators in the sea.

The teeth of the shortfin mako are long, slender, and slightly curved. They are visible even when the shark's mouth is closed.

SHORTFIN MAKO SHARK

ISURUS OXYRINCHUS

Habitat: Tropical, temperate offshore waters; Worldwide
Length: 3.9 m (13 ft)
Weight: 60–140 kg (130–308 lb)
Diet: Fish such as mackerel and swordfish, squid, marine mammals, other sharks, turtles
Lifespan: 30 years

Dangerous Meal

The shortfin mako hunts by soaring vertically from beneath its prey and tearing chunks from the victim's sides and fins. They like to hunt swordfish—but they don't always come off best in these encounters. Some makos have been found with swordfish bills embedded in their head and gills.

The swordfish—the delicious yet dangerous prey of the shortfin mako shark.

The shortfin can use its speed to launch itself high up into the air, and will sometimes even land on and damage boats. These attacks often injure people, too.

Like the great white, this shark can keep its body temperature warmer than the water around it.

DID YOU KNOW? There have been 20 recorded shortfin attacks on boats. In one case, a mako's bite sank a boat in three minutes!

Oceanic Whitetip Sharks

This solitary, slow-moving, deep-ocean shark has been called the most dangerous of all the sharks. This is because it is usually the first on the scene when a boat sinks or a plane crashes into the sea. In fact, it has almost certainly attacked more humans than all other sharks combined.

Open Wide!

The whitetip likes to eat rays, bony fish, turtles, crustaceans, dolphins, and whale carcasses, and even trash dumped by humans. Its usual feeding method is to swim into a group of fish with an open mouth in order to eat as many as it can.

The whitetip has a stocky body and long, widely spaced, white-tipped fins.

A whitetip keeps its mouth slightly open as it swims.

Oceanic whitetips typically swim slowly, but they can move fast when they want.

Sea Dogs

Oceanic whitetips are sometimes called sea dogs, because they often behave a bit like dogs! When this shark is interested in something, it will approach it with caution while deciding whether or not to attack. These sharks also follow ships for long distances, like a dog following its owner.

The whitetip can become more aggressive when competing with other species for a large food source, such as a whale carcass. This often results in a feeding frenzy.

OCEANIC WHITETIP SHARK

CARCHARHINUS LONGIMANUS

Habitat: Deep, open oceans; Worldwide
Length: Up to 4 m (13 ft)
Weight: Around 90 kg (200 lb) but up to 170 kg (374 lb)
Diet: Squid, fish such as tuna and marlin, sharks, rays, marine mammals, and birds
Lifespan: 25 years

DID YOU KNOW? The sharks have black tips on their fins and tail when they are young. These turn white as the shark grows in size.

Hammerhead Sharks

One of the most unusual-looking of all the sharks is the hammerhead. Its eyes and nostrils are spaced wide apart, giving it a T-shaped head.

Stalking Prey

There are, in fact, nine different types of hammerhead shark, including the bonnethead and scalloped hammerhead. All hammerheads are nocturnal. They hunt at night by swimming close to the sea floor, silently stalking their prey.

No one knows why scalloped hammerheads hang out in groups. It can't be for protection, as they have no predators. Perhaps they just enjoy the company!

HAMMERHEAD SHARK

SPHYRNIDAE

Habitat: Temperate and tropical waters; Worldwide
Length: 1–6 m (3–20 ft)
Weight: 3–450 kg (6.5–1,000 lb)
Diet: Stingrays, squid, octopus, crustaceans
Lifespan: Up to 30 years

Wide Eyes

Why the hammer-shaped head? Some scientists say it guides the shark up and down, while others think that they use it as a way of pinning down stingrays to the seafloor. Most likely, the head shape helps them hunt—the electric sensors in their heads are spread out over a broader area.

A hammerhead's head shape may also give it better vision than other sharks.

The shape of a hammerhead shark's head is called a cephalofoil.

The hammerhead's jaws are smaller than most sharks' and can't open as wide. Its mouth is full of small, sharp teeth.

Hammerheads are at risk, as some humans hunt them for their fins.

DID YOU KNOW? Hammerheads are one of the few animals that can get a tan from being in the sun.

99

Snakes

Snakes are nature's ultimate "stealth" predators—sneaking up silently on their prey before striking with swift and deadly precision.

Slither and Strike

Unlike their near relation, the lizard, snakes have no legs, and they must use their long, muscular, flexible body both for movement and to hold their prey.

This is a rat snake, a type of constrictor, meaning that it kills its prey by crushing it.

This is a wagler's pit viper. It lies in wait on tree branches, waiting for prey to pass by. When it does, it bites down hard to inject venom.

DID YOU KNOW? In 2018, an enormous Burmese python weighing in at 14 kg (32 lb) attacked and ate a white-tailed deer that was even bigger than the snake itself!

A snake's exact diet depends on its species, but all types eat meat.

Open Wide!

This snake is eating a mouse. Snakes do not chew their food. Their flexible jaws enable them to swallow their prey whole. Large snakes can open their jaws so wide, they can even swallow pigs!

Snakes use their forked tongue to smell their prey. They also have ears—inside their head!

Some snakes have organs in their upper lip that enable them to "see" the heat given off by their prey.

WAGLER'S PIT VIPER

TROPIDOLAEMUS WAGLERI

Habitat: Lowland forests and some mangroves; Southeast Asia
Length: 50–100 cm (20–40 in)
Weight: 2.7 kg (6 lb)
Diet: Small mammals and birds
Lifespan: Up to 14 years in captivity

Cobras

Cobras are famous for their hood, which they inflate when angry or about to attack. They are also the only snakes in the world that build a nest for their young—just like birds, but on the ground!

Super Senses

As well as a strong sense of smell, cobras have excellent vision, and can even see in the dark. They can also sense tiny changes in temperature, which helps them to track their prey at night.

Watch Out!

Spitting cobras are the only snake in the world that can spit their venom. They aim the venom at the eyes of their victims and are accurate to about half their own length!

The Cape cobra lives in southern Africa. It can be aggressive, and its venom is powerful enough to kill a human within two to five hours of being bitten.

There are many species of cobra. The biggest of these—the king cobra—is the longest venomous snake in the world.

When a spitting cobra attacks, it forces liquid from small, foward-facing openings in the front of its sharp fangs.

Cobras use their forked tongue to smell prey animals nearby.

This snake is sometimes called a yellow cobra. Its shading ranges from pale yellow to dark brown.

To extend its hood, a cobra expands the ribs in its neck.

CAPE COBRA

NAJA NIVEA

Habitat: Grasslands and deserts; southern Africa
Length: 1.2–1.6 m (3.9–5.2 ft)
Weight 4–6 kg (9–13 lb)
Diet: Mice, lizards, birds, and other snakes
Lifespan: Up to 20 years

DID YOU KNOW? King cobras inject so much venom in a single bite, they can kill an elephant.

Coral Snakes

Coral snakes are small, bright, and highly venomous. Most live in underground burrows or in piles of logs or rotting leaves. Aquatic species of coral snake live in lakes and rivers.

Hold on Tight

The coral snake delivers its venom through a pair of small fangs in the front of its top jaw. Unlike other venomous snakes, it tends to hold on to the victim while biting, giving time for the venom to take effect.

This variety, known as Hemprich's coral snake, is found in South America.

Coral snakes are shy creatures. They rarely bite humans, but when they do, the venom paralyzes the breathing muscles and is usually fatal.

ARIZONA CORAL SNAKE

MICRUROIDES EURYXANTHUS

Habitat: Woodland, scrubland, and rocky mountainous areas; Arizona and New Mexico (US) and Mexico
Length: 40–50 cm (15–19 in)
Weight: 1.4–2.3 kg (2–5 lb)
Diet: Small snakes and lizards
Lifespan: Up to 7 years in captivity

Clever Mimicry

The harmless scarlet kingsnake mimics venomous coral snakes to deter predators from attacking. Locals learn to distinguish between the two with a rhyme: red to yellow, kill a fellow; red to black, venom lack.

Kingsnakes kill their prey by gripping it tightly and constricting its breath.

When faced with potential attackers, these snakes release a bad smell, which scares away predators!

This snake species spends much of its time underground, coming out after dark to hunt for prey.

DID YOU KNOW? When threatened, the coral snake often curls the tip of its tail. This confuses the attacker as to which end is its head.

105

Rattlesnakes

The rattlesnake gets its name from the rattle at the tip of its tail, which it shakes as a warning if it feels threatened.

Deadly Diamond

Of the many kinds of rattlesnakes, the most famous is the western diamondback, which is responsible for more attacks on humans in the US than any other snake—although their bites are rarely fatal.

The rattle is made up of hollow beads that click together when the tail is vibrated. The sound has been compared to the crackling sound of frying fat.

Strike a Pose

Before striking, rattlesnakes are coiled except for the front of their body, which is raised, and the rattle, which is buzzing. They can strike up to two thirds of their body length.

MOJAVE RATTLESNAKE

CROTALUS SCUTULATUS

Habitat: Deserts; Southwestern US, and central Mexico
Length: Up to 1.3 m (4.5 ft)
Weight: 2.7–9 kg (6–20 lbs)
Diet: Small rodents and lizards
Lifespan: 12–24 years

Rattlesnakes can inject different amounts of venom through their hollow fangs, depending on the size of the prey.

The venom not only stuns the prey, but also starts the digestive process by breaking down the animal's tissue.

The sidewinder rattlesnake gets its name from its unusual sideways method of moving across the desert sand.

DID YOU KNOW? Rattlesnakes have two pits under their nostrils to detect the heat given off by warm–blooded prey. The pits are so sensitive, the snake can work out the exact size and location of the animal.

Boas

Boa constrictors are large, nonvenomous snakes that kill by constricting (crushing) their prey until they suffocate. These predators spend much of their time in trees, waiting to ambush any passing prey. They have a particular taste for bats, which they grab out of the air as they fly by.

Boas spend much of their time alone, unless it is time for them to mate and reproduce.

Time to Wrestle

A female boa constrictor leaves a scent trail to attract males when she is ready to mate. Often, more than one male snake finds it, leading to wrestling matches between the males. The winner gets to mate with the female.

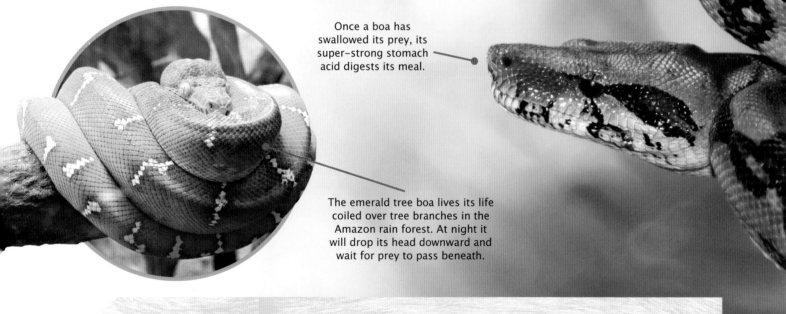

Once a boa has swallowed its prey, its super-strong stomach acid digests its meal.

The emerald tree boa lives its life coiled over tree branches in the Amazon rain forest. At night it will drop its head downward and wait for prey to pass beneath.

COMMON BOA	
BOA CONSTRICTOR IMPERATOR	**Habitat:** Rain forests and deserts; Central and South America **Length:** Up to 3 m (10 ft) **Weight:** Males 6-10 kg (15-23 lb), females 10-15 kg (22-33 lb) **Diet:** Rodents, lizards, mice, birds, bats, monkeys, wild pigs **Lifespan:** 25-30 years

DID YOU KNOW? Although they are around 50 cm (2 ft) long at birth, boas grow continually throughout their life.

These huge snakes spend most of their time in trees, but if they need to take to the water they are excellent swimmers.

Dinnertime!

Boas use heat sensors in their lips to locate warm-blooded prey. They have small, hooked teeth for grabbing and holding their victims while they wrap their coils around them and start to squeeze. It can take a boa six days to digest larger prey, after which it may not need to eat again for several months.

Boas are covered with cream, brown, and black oval and diamond patterns.

Anacondas

Anacondas are part of the boa family and are among the world's largest snakes. They are aquatic and live in and around the swamps and rivers of tropical South America. Like other boas, anacondas are constrictors—they kill their prey by crushing them to death in their coils.

Nocturnal Hunter

The anaconda hunts by night, feeding on fish, river birds, caimans, and mammals. It is an ambush predator, biting its prey and then enveloping the animal in its coils, squeezing until it suffocates. It then swallows its victim whole.

The green anaconda's dark green and black scales give it excellent camouflage in its swampy habitat.

Like the crocodile, the anaconda's nostrils are on top of its snout so it can breathe easily while swimming.

Anacondas sun themselves on branches close to rivers and streams so they can easily drop back into the water.

GREEN ANACONDA

EUNECTES MURINUS

Habitat: Swamps, marshes, rivers and streams; South America
Length: 6–9 m (19–29 ft)
Weight: 227 kg (550 lb)
Diet: Fish, small and large lizards, and mammals
Lifespan: 10 years

Anacondas spend most of their time lurking in slow-moving rivers or streams.

Snakes open their mouth wider than the width of their body!

A Big Meal

Anacondas can eat enormous animals, such as alligators and deer. Like all snakes, they have a special, flexible jaw that opens very wide, so they can swallow their prey whole. It can take several weeks to digest very large prey.

DID YOU KNOW? The heaviest anaconda on record weighed in at 227 kg (500 lb)! That's the weight of three adult humans!

Pythons

Pythons are large constrictor snakes dwelling in tropical and subtropical Asia, Africa, and Australia.

Adaptable Snakes

Pythons enjoy both wet and dry conditions and can swim and climb trees, increasing the number of potential prey. They can be bright green or dull brown, depending on what camouflages them best in their particular habitat.

Pythons, like boas, are ambush predators, remaining motionless in camouflaged positions before striking suddenly at passing prey. The largest of them have been known to eat animals as big as pigs and deer.

Green tree pythons have vivid green scales to camouflage them against the rain forest canopy where they live and hunt.

Pythons can open their mouth wide enough to eat large prey, such as this antelope.

DID YOU KNOW? The world record for longest snake is held by a python found in Celebes, Indonesia, in 1912. It measured exactly 10 m (33 ft).

GREEN TREE PYTHON

MORELIA VIRIDIS

Habitat: Tropical rain forests; Asia, Africa, Australia
Length: 1.5 m (5 ft)
Weight: Males up to 1.4 kg (3 lb), females up to 1.6 kg (3.5 lb)
Diet: Small mammals and lizards
Lifespan: 15–20 years

Green tree pythons look remarkably similar to emerald tree boas, even though they aren't closely related.

Egg Layers

A baby python emerges from its shell. Unlike boas, which bear live young, female pythons lay eggs. They keep the eggs warm by causing their muscles to shiver, raising their own body temperature.

Green tree pythons have prehensile (gripping) tails, which enable them to climb trees and grab onto prey.

Spiders

Spiders may be scary-looking beasts, yet humans have little to fear from most spiders. But in the bug world, spiders are deadly and fearsome predators.

Often kept as pets, Colombian giant tarantulas have a legspan of around 17 cm (7 in).

Amazing Arachnids

Spiders are not insects. They belong to a group of creatures called arachnids, which also includes scorpions, mites, and ticks.

Magnolia green jumping spiders can leap distances up to four times their body length!

A Deadly Bite

Most spiders kill or paralyze their prey by injecting venom. They then pump the victim's body with digestive juices that turn its insides to liquid. The spider sucks up the liquid, leaving an empty husk behind.

This jumping spider is sinking its fangs into the soft body of its prey.

COLOMBIAN GIANT TARANTULA

MEGAPHOBEMA ROBUSTUM

Habitat: Tropical rain forests; Colombia and Brazil, South America
Length: 15–20 cm (6–8 in)
Weight: Up to 175 g (6 oz)
Diet: Large insects
Lifespan: 1–2 years on average, but tarantulas can live up to 25 years in captivity.

The hairy legs of a Colombian giant tarantula are rusty orange, while its body is dark brown.

The hairs of this spider can cause a severe skin irritation if touched.

Tarantulas are large, hairy spiders that live in warm climates. Some can look monstrous and can be the size of dinner plates, but they rarely bite humans.

DID YOU KNOW? There are about 40,000 spider species that we know about, and probably thousands more that we haven't discovered yet.

Black Widows and Redbacks

Widow spiders are found in many of the warmer regions of the world. Two of the most famous kinds are the black widow spider, which lives in the desert regions of the southwestern United States, and the redback, which lives in Australia. These deadly spiders are closely related. The females of both species look quite similar.

The black widow spins cobwebs—messy tangles of sticky silken threads. Its silk is among the strongest of all spider silks.

Deadly Bite

The black widow is possibly the most venomous spider in North America. Its venom is 15 times more toxic than that of a rattlesnake. Yet it rarely kills humans because it injects only a tiny amount of poison when it bites. Only the female black widow is dangerous to humans.

Adult black widows are a glossy black but spiderlings are orange or brown.

BLACK WIDOW

LATRODECTUS MACTANS

Habitat: Dry places including rocks, logs and buildings; North America, Mexico and South America
Length: 2.4–4 cm (1–1.5 in).
Weight: Around 1 g (0.035 oz)
Diet: Insects such as ants, cockroaches, and beetles
Lifespan: 18 months

The female black widow guards her egg case. Each case contains hundreds of eggs.

The black widow doesn't have great eyesight. Instead, it feels the vibrations caused by the insect's body landing on its web.

Australian Black Widow

The redback is regarded as one of the most dangerous spiders in Australia. It has been known to eat animals as large as trapdoor spiders and lizards.

The redback is mainly nocturnal, waking each night to trap and eat its prey.

It builds its webs on the underside of ledges, rocks, and plants. Then it hangs upside down and waits for an insect to wander in.

DID YOU KNOW? Female black widows will sometimes kill and eat the male after they mate. Redback females have even been known to start eating the male while they are still mating!

Trapdoor Spiders

The trapdoor spider does not build a web. Instead it uses its powerful jaws to dig a tube-shaped burrow in the earth, which it lines with silk.

Lying in Wait

The trapdoor spider puts its front pair of legs against the trapdoor and waits. The hairs on its body are very sensitive to vibration.

When an insect wanders by, it feels the vibration, and shoots out of its burrow to catch it—biting down hard with its sharp fangs.

A trapdoor spider emerges from its burrow. Despite its eight eyes, it has poor eyesight, and relies on its sensitivity to vibration to catch its prey.

Clever Camouflage

It closes the burrow entrance with a trapdoor, using silk as a hinge, and plant and soil materials to camouflage it.

These spiders remain inside their tunnels unless it is time to hunt.

The burrow of a trapdoor spider can be as deep as 15 cm (6 in) long.

DID YOU KNOW? Trapdoor spiders are preyed on by spider wasps. When the wasp finds a burrow, she paralyzes the spider with her sting, then lays an egg on the body. When the egg hatches, the larva eats the spider alive.

Some types of trapdoor spider lay silken "trip lines" around their burrow. When an insect disturbs one of these lines, the spider is alerted, and rushes out.

The trapdoor spider has special teeth for digging.

It takes a trapdoor spider 6 to 12 hours to dig its burrow.

TRAPDOOR SPIDER

CTENIZIDAE

Habitat: Tropical regions worldwide
Length: Up to 4 cm (1.6 in)
Weight: 130 g (4.5 oz)
Diet: Insects, snakes, mice, small birds and frogs
Lifespan: 5–20 years

Tarantulas

The tarantula is feared by many people because of its large, hairy legs and body. This spider is, however, virtually harmless to humans. Its bite may be painful, but its venom is milder than a bee's.

Bird-Eater

Most tarantulas live in burrows, but some live in trees in a silken tube-shaped "tent." They hunt at night, feeding mainly on insects, although larger tarantulas target bigger prey, including frogs, lizards, mice, and even small snakes. The bird-eating spider, as its name suggests, sometimes feeds on young birds, which it steals from nests.

These large spiders use their body weight as a form of attack.

This tarantula is hiding in its burrow, awaiting its next meal.

CHILEAN ROSE HAIR TARANTULA

GRAMMOSTOLA ROSEA

Habitat: Desert and scrublands; Chile, Bolivia and Argentina, South America
Length: Up to 13 cm (5 in)
Weight: 55–85 g (2–3 oz)
Diet: Insects, mice, lizards, small snakes, young birds, and frogs
Lifespan: 20 years

DID YOU KNOW? When threatened by another animal, tarantulas kick off a cloud of tiny, hooked hairs from their abdomen. The hairs land on the animal's skin, making it feel itchy and sore.

It takes 3-4 years for Chilean rose tarantulas to grow to their adult size.

Tarantulas are found in tropical and desert regions of the world, including South America, southern Europe, Africa, southern Asia, and Australia.

The hairs on the body and legs of a Chilean rose hair tarantula are a reddish-pink—hence its name!

Experts believe that there are more than 850 different tarantula species.

The Biggest of All!

The biggest tarantula—and also the world's biggest spider—is the goliath spider, which can be up to 12 cm (5 in) long, and 27 cm (11 in) across. It lives in the coastal rain forests of South America.

A tarantula eats a grasshopper. The spider's venomous bite paralyzes its victim. Then it pours digestive juices into the grasshopper's body. This turns the insect's inner organs into a liquid soup, which the tarantula then sucks up.

121

Funnel-Web Spiders

Funnel-webs are highly venomous spiders found in southeastern Australia. The most infamous of these is the Sydney funnel-web, which can be very aggressive and has caused a number of human deaths.

Hooks and Fangs

A bite from a funnel-web spider can make someone very ill. Without medical attention, it can even kill. The spider's large, powerful fangs are strong enough to penetrate fingernails and soft shoes.

When a male funnel-web finds a female's burrow, he taps out a signal to tell her he wishes to mate with her. The female may well prefer to eat him, however. To stop the female's fangs from striking during mating, the male must use hooks on his second pair of legs to hold onto the female.

The Sydney funnel-web spider is regarded as one of the most dangerous spiders in the world. It will attack if it feels threatened.

Unusually for spiders, the male is more dangerous than the female.

The poweful fangs of a funnel-web spider point straight down.

FUNNEL-WEB SPIDERS

ATRACIDAE

Habitat: Moist forested areas; southeastern Australia
Length: 1–5 cm (0.4–2 in)
Weight: Up to 130 g (4.5 oz)
Diet: Beetles, snails, cockroaches, and other insects
Lifespan: Males 4 years; females 10 years or more

Scientists think venom from the funnel-web spider may have medical uses.

Female funnel-web spiders rarely leave their nests, whereas the males wander in search of mates.

Amazing Webs

Like the trapdoor spider, the funnel-web builds itself a silk-lined burrow, although it leaves this open rather than closing it with a trapdoor. At the front of the web is a flat surface—the perfect place to catch and devour prey.

A funnel-web spider lies in wait for prey.

DID YOU KNOW? Funnel-web venom is extremely toxic to humans and other primates, but is harmless to other mammals, such as cats and dogs.

Hunting Spiders

Some spiders don't sit and wait for their prey to come to them, but actively hunt. These include the wolf spider and the spitting spider.

Fast Runners

The wolf spider lives in burrows and hunts at night. It will lurk in a concealed spot and wait for its victim to come near, then chase it down. Some wolf spiders even jump in the air to catch flying insects.

A wolf spider feeds on a centipede. The spider's excellent eyesight and high sensitivity to vibrations make it an effective hunter.

A spitting spider fires its sticky spit to capture prey.

Spitting Spider

The spitting spider has a unique way of hunting. The spider's venom glands also produce a sticky kind of silk, which it spits at its victims.

As it spits it sways from side to side so that the spit comes out in two zigzags—one from each fang. These strings of spit glue the victim to the spot. The spider then moves in and gives its immobilized prey a venomous bite.

DID YOU KNOW? A spitting spider attack lasts just a little under 1/700th of a second.

On a good night a wolf spider can catch and eat up to 15 insects.

Unlike other spider species, the mother wolf spider carries her egg sac around with her, attached to the end of her abdomen.

The mother wolf spider can hunt, even while carrying her egg sac!

WOLF SPIDERS

LYCOSIDAE

Habitat: Grasslands, gardens, woodlands, farms; worldwide except Antarctica
Length: Up to 3 cm (1.2 in) long
Weight: Less than 30 g (1 oz)
Diet: Other spiders and insects including beetles, crickets, and grasshoppers
Lifespan: 1–2 years

Glossary

AMBUSH
Predators that use ambush tactics sit and wait for their prey before attacking.

AMPHIBIAN
Amphibians are typically small, backboned animals that require a watery environment to survive, such as frogs and toads.

AMPULLAE OF LORENZINI
Special organs that can sense low levels of electricity .

ARACHNIDS
The animal group that includes spiders, ticks, and mites.

ARCHIPELAGO
A group or chain of islands typically formed by volcanoes.

BILLABONG
A small body of water that is left behind when a river changes course.

BLUBBER
The layer of fat found in marine mammals such as seals.

BRACKISH WATER
Water that isn't as salty as seawater, but that is saltier than freshwater.

CANINE
A canine tooth is a long, pointed tooth used for tearing food.

CARCASS
An animal's dead body.

CARNIVORE
A carnivore eats meat only; an animal that eats other animals.

CARRION
The flesh of a dead animal. Animals that eat carrion won't have hunted the animal, and instead will have come across it in the wild.

CARTILAGE
Cartilage is a tough but flexible body tissue that makes up part or all of a skeleton.

COASTAL
The area of land that meets the sea.

COLD-BLOODED
If an animal's body temperature varies depending on its environment, it is called cold-blooded.

CONSTRICTOR
A constrictor is any animal that kills its prey by squeezing it to death.

CREEK
A shallow stream.

CROCODILIAN
The animal family that includes crocodiles, alligators, gharials, and caimans.

CRUSTACEAN
Crustaceans are animals such as crabs and lobsters. They have external skeletons, called exoskeletons.

EXTINCTION
When there are no more living members of a particular species, that species is said to be extinct. The process of a group dying out is called extinction.

FANGS
Long, sharp teeth which predators use to bite prey. In snakes and spiders, the fangs are sometimes used to inject venom into prey.

FRESHWATER
Bodies of freshwater have minimal levels of salt and include lakes, rivers, and ponds.

HABITAT
An animal's natural living environment.

HIBERNATION
The period an animal such as a bear spends in a dormant state over the cold winter months.

LIVESTOCK
Animals such as sheep, goats, and cattle that are farmed are called livestock.

MAMMAL
Animals in the mammal animal group have fur or hair. Female mammals typically give birth to live young and feed with milk that they produce.

MANGROVES
Trees and bushes that grow along seashores, forming swampy areas.

NOCTURNAL
Most active at night.

OMNIVORE
An omnivore eats both plants and meat.

PARALYZE
To cause something, such as a body part, to become immobile.

PREDATOR
An animal that preys on (hunts) another animal.

PREHENSILE
Grasping or gripping. For example, some animals have prehensile tails that can grip onto branches.

PREY
An animal that is preyed on (or hunted by) another animal.

PRIDE
A family group of lions is called a pride .

REPTILE
Reptiles are animals that have a backbone and scaly skin, such as snakes, crocodiles, and turtles. They are cold-blooded, which means they cannot regulate their body temperature. Typically, they lay eggs with soft shells.

SAVANNA
A grassy plain often with a few trees, found in tropical and subtropical areas.

SCRUBLAND
An area of land covered in shrubs, bushes, and small trees.

SUB-SAHARAN
The area of Africa below the Sahara Desert, which is found in the north of the continent.

SUBTROPICAL
Bordering on the tropics.

TROPICAL
Around the middle of the Earth at its widest point is an invisible line called the Equator. The areas just above and below this line are referred to as tropical or part of the tropics.

VENOMOUS
A venomous animal can inject a poisonous substance into the body of another animal.

Index